# Can You See Me?

I Like to Read® books, created by award-winning picture book artists as well as talented newcomers, instill confidence and the joy of reading in new readers.

We want to hear every new reader say, "I like to read!"

Visit our website for flash cards and activities:
www.holidayhouse.com/ILiketoRead
#ILTR
This book has been tested by an educational expert and determined to be a guided reading level C.

ALSO BY TED LEWIN

## Look!

★"A satisfying challenge and a fun animal adventure made thrilling by Lewin's characteristically spectacular use of light."
—*Kirkus Reviews* (starred review)

## What Am I? Where Am I?

# Can You See Me?

## by Ted Lewin

I Like to Read®

HOLIDAY HOUSE • NEW YORK

We live in the rain forest.

I am a bird.
Can you see me?

I am a snake.
Can you see me?

I am a sloth.
Can you
see me?

I am a reptile.
Can you
see me?

I am an otter.
Can you see me?

I am a bird.
Can you
see me?

I am a monkey.
Can you see me?

19

I am a crab.
Can you see me?

I am a lizard.
I am hard to see.

I am a bird.
You will *never* see me.

I am a frog.
I am small,
but I am easy to see.

We are still here.

TOUCAN

VINE SNAKE

TWO-TOED SLOTH

SPECTACLED CAIMAN

RIVER OTTER

TIGER HERON

HOWLER MONKEY

LAND CRAB

BASILISK LIZARD

GREAT POTOO

RED POISON DART FROG

*For my guide,*
*Fernando, who sees everything*

*Special thanks to Michael and Yolanda Kaye,*
*Tortuga Lodge.*

I LIKE TO READ is a registered trademark of Holiday House Publishing, Inc.

Copyright © 2014 by Ted Lewin
All Rights Reserved
HOLIDAY HOUSE is registered in the U.S. Patent and Trademark Office.
Printed and Bound in September 2018 at Tien Wah Press, Johor Bahru, Johor, Malaysia.
The artwork was created with pencil, watercolor, and liquid mask on Strathmore bristol.
www.holidayhouse.com
7 9 10 8 6

Library of Congress Cataloging-in-Publication Data
Lewin, Ted.
Can you see me? / by Ted Lewin. — First edition.
pages cm. — (I like to read)
Audience: K to grade 3.
ISBN 978-0-8234-2940-0 (hardcover)
1. Rain forest animals—Juvenile literature.  I. Title.
QL112.L49 2014
591.734—dc23
2013009555

ISBN 978-0-8234-3299-8 (paperback)

I Like to Read® Books in Paperback
You will like all of them!

*Bad Dog* by David McPhail
*The Big Fib* by Tim Hamilton
*Boy, Bird, and Dog* by David McPhail
*Can You See Me?* by Ted Lewin
*Car Goes Far* by Michael Garland
*Come Back, Ben* by Ann Hassett and John Hassett
*The Cowboy* by Hildegard Müller
*Dinosaurs Don't, Dinosaurs Do* by Steve Björkman
*Ed and Kip* by Kay Chorao
*The End of the Rainbow* by Liza Donnelly
*Fireman Fred* by Lynn Rowe Reed
*Fish Had a Wish* by Michael Garland
*The Fly Flew In* by David Catrow
*Good Night, Knight* by Betsy Lewin
*Grace* by Kate Parkinson
*Happy Cat* by Steve Henry
*I Have a Garden* by Bob Barner
*I Said, "Bed!"* by Bruce Degen
*I Will Try* by Marilyn Janovitz
*Late Nate in a Race* by Emily Arnold McCully
*The Lion and the Mice* by Rebecca Emberley and Ed Emberley
*Little Ducks Go* by Emily Arnold McCully
*Look!* by Ted Lewin
*Look Out, Mouse!* by Steve Björkman
*Me Too!* by Valeri Gorbachev
*Mice on Ice* by Rebecca Emberley and Ed Emberley
*Pete Won't Eat* by Emily Arnold McCully
*Pig Has a Plan* by Ethan Long
*Ping Wants to Play* by Adam Gudeon
*Sam and the Big Kids* by Emily Arnold McCully
*See Me Dig* by Paul Meisel
*See Me Run* by Paul Meisel
A THEODOR SEUSS GEISEL AWARD HONOR BOOK
*Sick Day* by David McPhail
*3, 2, 1, Go!* by Emily Arnold McCully
*What Am I? Where Am I?* by Ted Lewin
*You Can Do It!* by Betsy Lewin

Visit http://www.holidayhouse.com/I-Like-to-Read/ for more about I Like to Read® books, including flash cards, reproducibles, and the complete list of titles.